1 AND THESSALONIANS

Stand Firm
in Faith

A Guided Discovery for Groups and Individuals

Paul Thigpen

LOYOLAPRESS.
CHICAGO

LOYOLAPRESS.

3441 N. ASHLAND AVENUE
CHICAGO, ILLINOIS 60657
(800) 621-1008
WWW.LOYOLABOOKS.ORG

Nihil Obstat	*Imprimatur*
Reverend John G. Lodge, S.S.L., S.T.D.	Most Reverend Edwin M. Conway, D.D.
Censor Deputatus	Vicar General
March 29, 2004	Archdiocese of Chicago
	March 31, 2004

The Scripture quotations contained herein are from the New Revised Standard Version Bible: Catholic Edition, copyright © 1993 and 1989 by the Division of Christian Education of the National Council of the Churches of Christ in the U.S.A. Used by permission. All rights reserved. Subheadings in Scripture quotations have been added by Paul Thigpen.

The original Greek text of St. John Chrysostom's homilies can be found in several editions; the excerpt on page 21, translated by Paul Thigpen, is based on the Second Benedictine edition of his works, *Ioannou Chrysostomou . . .* , Bernard de Montfacon, ed. (Paris: Apud Gaume fratres, 1834–39).

"Marcel Van: Refined by Fire" (p. 31) is drawn from the biographical sketch in Paul Thigpen, *Blood of the Martyrs, Seed of the Church: Stories of Catholics Who Died for Their Faith* (Ann Arbor, Mich.: Charis Books, 2001), 190–94.

The prayer of St. Thomas Aquinas (p. 40) is from *The Manual of Catholic Prayer for All Days and Seasons and Every Circumstance of Christian Life* (New York: Harper and Row, 1961), 18.

The excerpt from the Dogmatic Constitution on Divine Revelation (p. 41) is taken from Walter M. Abbott, S.J., ed., *The Documents of Vatican II* (New York: Guild Press, 1966), 115.

The language of the original sixteenth-century English text of St. Thomas More was modernized by Paul Thigpen for the excerpt on page 50. Several editions of the original are available, including Thomas More, *The Godly Instructions and Prayers of Blessed Sir Thomas More, Written in the Tower of London, 1535* (Worcester: Stanbrook Abbey, 1922).

The Catechism excerpt (p. 60) is from the English translation of the *Catechism of the Catholic Church* for use in the United States of America, Second Edition, copyright © 1994, 1997, United States Catholic Conference, Inc.—Libreria Editrice Vaticana. Used with permission.

The original Greek text of St. Athanasius' discourses can be found in Edward W. Bright, ed., *Orations against the Arians* (Oxford: Oxford University Press, 1872). The excerpt on page 61 was translated by Paul Thigpen.

"What's This 'Rapture' Stuff All About?" (p. 72–75) is drawn from Paul Thigpen, *The Rapture Trap: A Catholic Response to End Times Fever* (West Chester, Pa.: Ascension, 2001).

Interior design by Kay Hartmann/Communique Design
Illustration by Charise Mericle Harper

ISBN 0-8294-2009-6

Printed in the United States of America
04 05 06 07 08 09 10 Bang 10 9 8 7 6 5 4 3 2 1

Contents

How to Use This Guide

You might compare the Bible to a national park. The park is so large that you could spend months, even years, getting to know it. But a brief visit, if carefully planned, can be enjoyable and worthwhile. In a few hours you can drive through the park and pull over at a handful of sites. At each stop you can get out of the car, take a short trail through the woods, listen to the wind blowing through the trees, get a feel for the place.

In this booklet, we will read Paul's two letters to the Christian community of Thessalonica. Because the excerpts are short, we will be able to take a leisurely walk through them, thinking carefully about what we are reading and what Paul's words mean for our lives.

This guide provides everything you need to explore 1 and 2 Thessalonians in six discussions—or to do a six-part exploration on your own. The introduction on page 6 will prepare you to get the most out of your reading. The weekly sections provide explanations that will help illuminate the significance of Paul's words for today. Equally important, each section supplies questions that will launch your group into fruitful discussion, helping you to both investigate the letters for yourself and learn from one another. If you're using the booklet by yourself, the questions will spur your personal reflection.

Each discussion is meant to be a *guided discovery*.

Guided. None of us is equipped to read the Bible without help. We read the Bible *for* ourselves but not *by* ourselves. Scripture was written to be understood and applied in the community of faith. So each week "A Guide to the Reading," drawing on the work of both modern biblical scholars and Christian writers of the past, supplies background and explanations. The guide will help you grasp the meanings of 1 and 2 Thessalonians. Think of it as a friendly park ranger who points out noteworthy details and explains what you're looking at so you can appreciate things for yourself.

Discovery. The purpose is for *you* to interact with these New Testament letters. "Questions for Careful Reading" is a tool to help you dig into the text and examine it carefully. "Questions for

Application" will help you consider what these words mean for your life here and now. Each week concludes with an "Approach to Prayer" section that helps you respond to God's word. Supplementary "Living Tradition" and "Saints in the Making" sections offer the thoughts and experiences of Christians past and present. By showing what these letters have meant to others, these sections will help you consider what they mean for you.

How long are the discussion sessions? We've assumed you will have about an hour and a half when you get together. If you have less time, you'll find that most of the elements can be shortened somewhat.

Is homework necessary? You will get the most out of your discussions if you read the weekly material and prepare your answers to the questions in advance of each meeting. If participants are not able to prepare, have someone read the "Guide to the Reading" sections aloud to the group at the points where they appear.

What about leadership? If you happen to have a world-class biblical scholar in your group, by all means ask him or her to lead the discussions. In the absence of any professional Scripture scholars, or even accomplished amateur biblical scholars, you can still have a first-class Bible discussion. Choose two or three people to take turns as facilitators, and have everyone read "Suggestions for Bible Discussion Groups" (page 76) before beginning.

Does everyone need a guide? a Bible? Everyone in the group will need his or her own copy of this booklet. It contains the complete text of 1 and 2 Thessalonians, so a Bible is not absolutely necessary for everyone—but each participant will find it useful to have one. Some of the questions call for reading passages of Scripture that are not included in this booklet. You should have at least one Bible on hand for your discussions. (See page 80 for recommendations.)

How do we get started? Before you begin, take a look at the suggestions for Bible discussion groups (page 76) or individuals (page 79).

Words of Wisdom, Words of Hope

In the Second Gulf War, several of my Catholic friends serving in the U.S. Army fought on the front lines in Iraq. One day I received some distressing news that one of them was suffering from low morale, his mind and heart deeply troubled by the relentless stresses of warfare and its aftermath. So I wrote him a long letter to offer encouragement, advice, and assurances of my prayers and support.

A few days later I learned that a former student in one of the university classes I once taught had embraced the Catholic faith, turning to God from a life of occult spiritual practices, alcohol abuse, and sexual promiscuity. But her convictions were still in their infancy, her moral thinking was confused, and her old friends—feeling betrayed by her transformation—were pressuring her to resume her old way of life. Since she lived in another city, I decided to write another long letter. I asked God to speak to her, through me, his words of comfort and hope, along with some practical wisdom for Christian living.

The situations that prompted me to write these Christian friends in need call to mind the circumstances that moved Paul to write his two letters to the Thessalonians. The ancient Christians of Thessalonica were not at war as my soldier friend was, yet they were nevertheless facing interior battles—spiritual, mental, and emotional—much like his. Hostile circumstances attacked their faith, captured their thoughts, exploded their peace of heart. They needed, as Paul put it, spiritual armor to defend themselves (1 Thessalonians 5:8).

The Thessalonians were also in some ways like my former student who had just converted to the Catholic faith. Apparently, many of them had only recently become Christians and had left behind a way of life common among their neighbors, a life given to worship in pagan cults, sexual license, and alcohol abuse. Their new faith was fragile, their spiritual understanding limited. They, too, faced powerful pressures and temptations to give up their convictions through the influence of old acquaintances and the surrounding culture. They needed, as Paul recognized, encouragement to stand firm in their conversion from idolatry, sexual immorality, and drunkenness (1 Thessalonians 1:9; 4:3; 5:6–8).

Yet another parallel appears here as well. The letters I wrote to my two friends were motivated not only by my love for them but also by a sense of responsibility. The soldier had taken part in a course on Scripture that I had taught, so I was eager to continue helping him cultivate his spiritual growth. A conversation I'd had years before with my former student had helped to plant the seeds of conversion in her life. So I was equally interested in nurturing her newly sprouting faith.

In a similar way, Paul loved the Thessalonians as dear friends, and he, too, felt a responsibility for their spiritual welfare. He had come to Thessalonica as a missionary pastor, calling people to faith in Jesus and establishing a local church there. The conversion of these new Christians was rooted in his preaching, and their growth in Christ afterward had been nourished by his teaching and example as he lived and worked among them.

Not surprisingly, then, Paul assumed a role as their spiritual father, and he was deeply concerned with pressing them toward spiritual maturity and warning them against dangers in their new life with God. When circumstances took him away from them to another city, he could no longer teach, counsel, and oversee the young church's affairs in person. So he quite naturally began a correspondence with them. Letters had to take the place of his personal presence in the community.

At least some of the challenges encountered by the church in Thessalonica are faced by all Christians from time to time, today as in Paul's day. Those who are new converts struggle to establish their faith firmly despite puzzling questions and the temptations of their former life. Those who have always been Christians face occasional doubts and powerful temptations as well. Social pressures squeeze us toward spiritual and moral compromises, or toward giving up our faith altogether.

At the same time, no Christian is completely free from the kinds of adversity that are common to all people: illness and bereavement, financial struggles, broken family ties, troubled personal relationships. Such difficulties often leave us under a weight of anxiety, doubt, discouragement, confusion, or even despair.

For all these reasons, the letters of Paul to the Thessalonians have much to say to us all. Whether two thousand years ago or today, God speaks to Christians through these words to bring wisdom and hope. At the same time, understanding something of the community life of those ancient believers and their relationship to their spiritual leader, Paul, can help us better understand ourselves as contemporary Christians who also seek to live together a life pleasing to God.

Before we delve more deeply into these letters, however, we need a little background.

Thessalonica (today known as Thessaloníki) is a large seaport in northern Greece. In Paul's day it lay at the crossroads of major highways running north, south, east, and west across the vast Roman Empire, making it an important and prosperous city. Thessalonica teemed with people of diverse ethnic backgrounds from Europe, Asia, and Africa. The city also displayed a wide variety of religious traditions: worship of traditional Greek, Roman, and Egyptian gods; the civil religion of the empire, which considered the emperor divine; cults whose frenzied rituals centered on alcohol and sex; and a Jewish community.

Into this complex, bustling urban setting Paul arrived as a Christian missionary pastor sometime around AD 50. The apostle (from a Greek word that means literally "someone sent out") was himself a convert. Before his missionary journeys, he had been a devout Jewish religious leader who had viewed the new Christian movement—made up mostly of fellow Jews—as a spiritual and social threat to the established traditions of his people. For that reason, Paul had actually persecuted the Christians in Jerusalem and other towns.

One day, however, a powerful encounter with the risen Christ in a vision convinced him that this Jesus whom he had opposed was in fact savior and lord, not only of the Jews but of the whole world (Acts 9:1–19; 22:1–21). After that sudden and startling conversion, Paul dedicated himself to preaching the Good News, or "gospel," about Jesus, traveling from city to city, calling everyone to repentance and faith, whether Jews or gentiles (non-Jews). In each city where he preached, he organized a church community.

Since the apostle felt compelled by God to take the gospel throughout the empire, he couldn't settle down permanently in any one city. So he continued to care for his new converts as he traveled by writing them letters of inspiration, encouragement, and doctrinal and moral instruction. Several of these letters have survived—1 Thessalonians is the earliest of them—and they now form part of the New Testament in our Bible.

Biblical scholars have long debated where Paul was staying when he wrote to the Thessalonian church, how much time elapsed between the writing of the two letters to Thessalonica, and exactly what happened in the meantime. Using clues from other biblical texts, some have concluded that he wrote from the Greek city of Corinth, whose young church the apostle had also founded (later the Corinthian Christians received from him the letters we now know as the biblical books of 1 and 2 Corinthians). Other scholars speculate that he was staying in the Greek city of Athens. One estimate would place Paul in Thessalonica for three or four months in the first part of the year 50. He would have written the first letter about four or five months after he left the city, toward the end of the year, and would have written the second letter several months later, in the early part of 51.

For various reasons, some modern scholars have challenged the idea that these letters were produced by Paul, suggesting instead that other early Christians wrote them using his name. Nearly all biblical scholars today, however, are agreed that the first letter was indeed composed by the apostle. A number of them agree as well that the second letter was also genuinely his. The Church Fathers insisted even in the early centuries of the Christian era—much closer to Paul's own time—that both these letters are authentic writings of the apostle, and this traditional view will be the basis of our discussion in this book.

To provide some additional scriptural background for Paul's letters to the Thessalonians, an account of his first visit to their city is included in our reading for Week 2. It comes from the Acts of the Apostles, the second portion of a longer work whose first part is the Gospel of Luke. According to ancient tradition, this Gospel writer was the physician named Luke who sometimes accompanied Paul on his journeys (Colossians 4:14). Though Luke did not go with Paul to Thessalonica, he nevertheless included in his history some events of that particular mission.

The apostle spent his time in Thessalonica pouring himself into the task of building a Christian community. He instructed the new believers in the basics of the faith with compelling preaching about the life, death, resurrection, and second coming of Christ. He drew insights from Jewish moral teachings and the life of Jesus to help them understand how to please God in their daily living. He likely followed the typical pattern of his ministry described in other New Testament books, which included providing the sacraments of baptism (Acts 16:14–15; 1 Corinthians 1:14–16) and the Eucharist (1 Corinthians 10:15–18), establishing liturgical worship (1 Corinthians 11:23–26; Colossians 3:16; 1 Timothy 2:1–2; 4:13), and ordaining leadership (1 Timothy 3:1–13).

During his months in Thessalonica, the apostle offered a moving personal example for the community that motivated them to sacrificial love and service. No wonder, then, that the Thessalonian Christians loved their spiritual father intensely, felt orphaned when he was forced to leave the city, and longed to see him again (1 Thessalonians 3:6). For his part, Paul also grieved deeply over the separation and grew desperately anxious over the well-being of his spiritual children, given that they were still so young in their new faith.

His concern was sharpened by the knowledge that the Christians in Thessalonica were surrounded by hostility from their neighbors. A mob had forced Paul to flee the city; had the mob attacked his little flock again? Had the local authorities continued to harass them? Were the believers being ostracized in the workplace or denounced and rejected by friends and family members? Would they be able to stand firm against such opposition, or would they despair, lose faith, and return to their old way of life?

Paul's anxiety intensified. At last he sent his colleague Timothy back to Thessalonica to encourage the church and inquire about its welfare (1 Thessalonians 2:17–3:5). Here is an outline of the situation Timothy apparently reported when he returned:

As a whole, the new community was standing firm and even growing. Despite continuing opposition, the Thessalonian

Christians remained faithful and were zealous in evangelizing many of their neighbors. This good news brought Paul considerable joy and relief (1 Thessalonians 1:2–10; 3:6–8).

Nevertheless, questions had arisen over the implications of the apostle's teaching. Several issues needed his clarification (1 Thessalonians 3:10; 4:13).

Tensions had emerged within the community because of misunderstood prophetic utterances and church members who were idle busybodies (1 Thessalonians 4:11–12; 5:19–21). They needed some gentle but firm correction, as well as warnings to respect their spiritual leaders and maintain peace among themselves (1 Thessalonians 5:12–13).

Temptations were strong to return to old behavior patterns. The new converts had to be reminded that God was calling them to higher standards of conduct than those held by the culture surrounding them (1 Thessalonians 4:2–8; 5:4–11, 15, 22).

The apostle's letter no doubt improved the situation in Thessalonica considerably. Even so, some time later he apparently learned that a few of the problems had continued or even grown worse. So a second letter was called for, dealing with many of the same themes but approaching them from a different angle.

Because the two letters overlap in content and have a similar structure, we will study them alongside each other in stereo rather than one at a time. Doing so will allow us to make some useful comparisons between them and also to recognize the recurring nature of many challenges to living the Christian life.

Meanwhile, throughout our study, we should keep in mind Paul's exhortation to "stand firm in the Lord" (1 Thessalonians 3:8). Sooner or later, doubt, confusion, temptation, opposition, and other adversities will come our way. When that happens, we can turn to the enduring message in these letters, for they are written to us as well. The apostle's words echo down the centuries to strengthen us: "Now may our Lord Jesus Christ himself and God our Father, who loved us and through grace gave us eternal comfort and good hope, comfort your hearts and strengthen them in every good work and word" (2 Thessalonians 2:16–17).

THE MESSENGERS ARE THE MESSAGE

Questions to Begin

15 minutes
Use a question or two to get warmed up for the reading.

---

1 Have you ever received good news in a phone call, letter, or e-mail that changed your life? If so, what was the news, and how did it arrive?

---

2 What is the most memorable welcome you have ever received?

1. Letter in Spain –
– Received grad. assistantship

2. Danthauz – beyond the horizon award

Opening the Bible

5 minutes
Read the passage aloud. Let individuals take turns reading
sections.

The Reading: 1 Thessalonians 1:1–10;
2 Thessalonians 1:1–12

Paul Writes His Friends in Thessalonica: "Thank God for You!"

1 Thessalonians 1:1 Paul, Silvanus, and Timothy,
To the church of the Thessalonians in God the Father and the
Lord Jesus Christ:
Grace to you and peace.
2 We always give thanks to God for all of you and mention you
in our prayers, constantly 3 remembering before our God and Father
your work of faith and labor of love and steadfastness of hope in our
Lord Jesus Christ. 4 For we know, brothers and sisters beloved by
God, that he has chosen you, 5 because our message of the gospel
came to you not in word only, but also in power and in the Holy
Spirit and with full conviction; just as you know what kind of persons
we proved to be among you for your sake. 6 And you became
imitators of us and of the Lord, for in spite of persecution you
received the word with joy inspired by the Holy Spirit, 7 so that you
became an example to all the believers in Macedonia and in Achaia.
8 For the word of the Lord has sounded forth from you not only in
Macedonia and Achaia, but in every place your faith in God has
become known, so that we have no need to speak about it. 9 For the
people of those regions report about us what kind of welcome we
had among you, and how you turned to God from idols, to serve a
living and true God, 10 and to wait for his Son from heaven, whom
he raised from the dead—Jesus, who rescues us from the wrath that
is coming.

Several Months Later Paul Writes Again:
"We're Praying for You!"

2 Thessalonians 1:1 Paul, Silvanus, and Timothy,
To the church of the Thessalonians in God our Father and the
Lord Jesus Christ:
2 Grace to you and peace from God our Father and the Lord
Jesus Christ.
3 We must always give thanks to God for you, brothers and
sisters, as is right, because your faith is growing abundantly, and the

love of everyone of you for one another is increasing. 4 Therefore we ourselves boast of you among the churches of God for your steadfastness and faith during all your persecutions and the afflictions that you are enduring.

5 This is evidence of the righteous judgment of God, and is intended to make you worthy of the kingdom of God, for which you are also suffering. 6 For it is indeed just of God to repay with affliction those who afflict you, 7 and to give relief to the afflicted as well as to us, when the Lord Jesus is revealed from heaven with his mighty angels 8 in flaming fire, inflicting vengeance on those who do not know God and on those who do not obey the gospel of our Lord Jesus. 9 These will suffer the punishment of eternal destruction, separated from the presence of the Lord and from the glory of his might, 10 when he comes to be glorified by his saints and to be marveled at on that day among all who have believed, because our testimony to you was believed. 11 To this end we always pray for you, asking that our God will make you worthy of his call and will fulfill by his power every good resolve and work of faith, 12 so that the name of our Lord Jesus may be glorified in you, and you in him, according to the grace of our God and the Lord Jesus Christ.

Questions for Careful Reading

10 minutes
Choose questions according to your interest and time.

1   Which key words and ideas appearing in the introductions of these two letters do you suspect might turn out to be prominent themes in the letters?

2   What do these passages indicate about the quality of the relationship between Paul and the Thessalonian Christians? (Cite specific verses.)

3   Is Paul pleased with the Thessalonians?

4   What does Paul tell us about Jesus in these passages: 1 Thessalonians 1:1, 3, 10; 2 Thessalonians 1:1–2, 7–12?

5   What is Paul talking about when he speaks of "the punishment of eternal destruction, separated from the presence of the Lord" (2 Thessalonians 1:9)?

A Guide to the Reading

If participants have not read this section already, read it aloud. Otherwise go on to "Questions for Application."

1 Thessalonians 1:1; 2 Thessalonians 1:1–2. The greetings in both letters remind us that Paul rarely ministers alone, recognizing the essential strength found in Christian fellowship. Timothy has traveled to a number of cities as a missionary colleague with Paul and has become his close friend. The two men worked together to establish the church in Thessalonica.

"Silvanus" is the Latin form of the name "Silas." The Silvanus mentioned here is most likely the Silas described in Acts, another companion of Paul on his missionary journeys who escaped with him by night from Thessalonica (Acts 17:10) and shared his beatings and imprisonment in the city of Philippi (Acts 16:19–40).

The apostle calls God "Father," right away reminding his readers both of God's loving care for them and of their spiritual kinship as brothers and sisters in God's family. In these two brief letters, when Paul refers to God, to the Thessalonian Christians, and to himself, he uses family relationship terms a remarkable fifty-two times. Having become a community only recently, drawn from various social classes and religious backgrounds, the Thessalonian Christians must build a new identity as "the household of God" (Ephesians 2:19). This identity is especially important for converts who are being rejected and denounced by members of their natural families for abandoning the traditional ways of their ancestors.

The phrase "grace to you and peace" (1 Thessalonians 1:1) is the blessing that Paul characteristically offers to fellow Christians and may have come from an early Christian liturgy. These words go straight to the heart of the gospel: by the *grace* of God—his extravagant, merciful goodness extended to us in Jesus as a free gift—we are offered *peace* with God, a healing of our broken relationship with him. Because we are now united to God in Christ, this grace is the very life of God within us, giving us the power to overcome sin so we can become like him and live with him forever.

1 Thessalonians 1:2–9; 2 Thessalonians 1:3–4. Paul expresses his delight in the new Christians at Thessalonica by thanking God for them in a number of specific ways. He rejoices that they endured and bore spiritual fruit despite persecution (1 Thessalonians 1:6; 2 Thessalonians 1:4). Through Paul's words of appreciation, God their Father is himself commending them, assuring them that they are "beloved" and "chosen" (1 Thessalonians 1:4).

Paul describes here an important pattern: as he, Timothy, and Silvanus worked and preached in Thessalonica, the people there found that these men's lives modeled the reality of their message. That model had "power"; it brought "full conviction" that their words were true (1 Thessalonians 1:5). As a result, the Thessalonians "turned to God from idols," becoming "imitators" of the missionaries (1 Thessalonians 1:6, 9).

Then the process repeated itself: the converts themselves became the kind of people who offer a compelling example to others, not only in their city but throughout the surrounding region. Faith gave birth to faith as the Thessalonians evangelized their neighbors (1 Thessalonians 1:5–9).

1 Thessalonians 1:10; 2 Thessalonians 1:5–12. To inspire even more "steadfastness of hope" (1 Thessalonians 1:3), Paul makes his first reference to a major topic in both letters: the second coming of Christ. These and other biblical passages indicate that God's "vengeance" when Jesus returns does not mean the kind of malicious retaliation for injury that human beings often seek. Instead, it refers to God's decisive and final response to the universal cry of the human heart for justice. Christ will come to stop the work of evildoers, pass "righteous judgment" (2 Thessalonians 1:5) on them, rescue their victims, and vindicate the innocent. He will set the world aright.

Paul speaks of those who reject God in the end as suffering "the punishment of eternal destruction" (2 Thessalonians 1:9). Whatever else the notion of eternal damnation might imply, the apostle zeros in on its most terrifying aspect: those who remain God's enemies will be "separated from the presence of the Lord" (2 Thessalonians 1:9). What could be worse than cutting yourself off forever from the very source of all life, goodness, beauty, and truth?

There are things in all of us, Paul says, that must be set aright; we must become just as God is just. So in light of Jesus' return as judge, he prays that God's grace will make them "worthy of his call and will fulfill by his power every good resolve and work of faith" (2 Thessalonians 1:11).

Questions for Application

40 minutes
Choose questions according to your interest and time.

"Actions speak louder
~than words"
What goes around comes around

1 Paul speaks of believers' "work of faith" (1 Thessalonians 1:3), implying that faith and works cannot be separated (compare James 2:14–26). How has your own experience illustrated that faith is inseparable from the way you live?

2 Can you recall a specific occasion when some particular truth of the gospel "came to you not in word only, but also in power and in the Holy Spirit and with full conviction" (1 Thessalonians 1:5)? Was it during Mass? in a conversation? during prayer or Scripture study? through the example of another person? What was it about the way the truth was presented that you found so compelling? What can you learn from that experience?

3 Which Christians have you known or read about who inspire you to become "imitators of [them] and of the Lord" (1 Thessalonians 1:6)? Why do they inspire you? What specifically about their example could you imitate this week?

4 Paul rejoices that "the word of the Lord has sounded forth" (1 Thessalonians 1:8) from the Thessalonians to others, suggesting that these new believers weren't shy about sharing the gospel. Do you talk openly with non-Christians about your faith? If not, what would make it easier for you to do so?

5 Even Paul, an extraordinarily gifted apostle, recognized his need for Christian fellowship and cooperation in service to the Christian community. In what concrete ways are you working with other Catholics to serve the Church?

The Emperor of heaven, the Lord of men and angels, has sent you his letters for your life's advantage. . . . Study them, I beg you, and meditate daily on the words of your Creator. Learn the heart of God in the words of God.

Pope St. Gregory the Great, *Letters*

Approach to Prayer

15 minutes
Use this approach—or create your own!

◆ Sometimes we tend to spend all our time with God making requests. In these letters, Paul shows how thanksgiving should also be a regular part of our conversations with the Lord.

The ancient Hebrews included among their psalms many beautiful hymns of thanksgiving and praise to God for his goodness. Have someone read aloud (or have everyone read aloud together) Psalm 100, a psalm of thanksgiving that has been a favorite of God's people for many centuries. Afterward, spend a few minutes in silent praise for the Lord's goodness to you. Then end with a Glory Be.

A Living Tradition

Genuine Love Means Loving Everyone

This section is a supplement for individual reading.

St. John Chrysostom, who lived about 347–407, was the patriarch (the equivalent of an archbishop) of the great city of Constantinople, the eastern capital of the ancient Roman Empire. He became famous for his preaching (*Chrysostom* is a title meaning "golden-mouthed" in Greek), gaining both enthusiastic admirers and deadly enemies through his straight-shooting critique of the culture and society of his day. Christians and pagans, rich and poor, commoners and even the empress herself were publicly corrected from his pulpit. The following thoughts come from his *First Homily on the Second Letter of St. Paul to the Thessalonians.*

The apostle says to the Thessalonians: "The love of everyone of you for one another is increasing" (2 Thessalonians 1:3). Observe closely this love among the Thessalonians. They did not love one person rather than another, but their love was equal toward all. . . .

Sometimes we find a certain kind of love among the people of a community, but it is a kind of love that leads to division. We knit ourselves together in parties of two or three, and these cliques are closely bound to one another but keep themselves apart from the rest, because they support and confide in no one outside their own little group. But this is not really love—it is the tearing apart of love. . . . If we confine to one or two people the love that ought to be extended to the whole Church of God, we injure both ourselves and them, and the whole community. . . .

What advantage is it if you love a certain person extravagantly? It is only a human love. But if you want a love that is not merely human—if you want to love for God's sake—then love everyone. For God has commanded us to love even our enemies. And if he has commanded us to love our enemies, how much more those who have never injured us?

Well, you may say, I love, but not in *that* way. In that case, you are not really loving at all.

WE NEVER SAID IT WOULD BE EASY

Questions to Begin

15 minutes
Use a question or two to get warmed up for the reading.

1 Name a historical figure (other than Jesus Christ) who in your opinion "turned the world upside down." What did he or she do that was so earthshaking?

2 If tomorrow you could visit someone far away whom you haven't seen for a long time, who would it be and why?

Opening the Bible

5 minutes
Read the passage aloud. Let individuals take turns reading
paragraphs.

The Reading: Acts 17:1–10, 13; 1 Thessalonians 2:1–20

A Tough Start for the Mission to Thessalonica

Acts 17:1 After Paul and Silas had passed through Amphipolis and
Apollonia, they came to Thessalonica, where there was a synagogue
of the Jews. 2 And Paul went in, as was his custom, and on three
sabbath days argued with them from the scriptures, 3 explaining and
proving that it was necessary for the Messiah to suffer and to rise
from the dead, and saying, "This is the Messiah, Jesus whom I am
proclaiming to you." 4 Some of them were persuaded and joined Paul
and Silas, as did a great many of the devout Greeks and not a few of
the leading women. 5 But the Jews became jealous, and with the help
of some ruffians in the marketplaces they formed a mob and set the
city in an uproar. While they were searching for Paul and Silas to
bring them out to the assembly, they attacked Jason's house. 6 When
they could not find them, they dragged Jason and some believers
before the city authorities, shouting, "These people who have been
turning the world upside down have come here also, 7 and Jason has
entertained them as guests. They are all acting contrary to the decrees
of the emperor, saying that there is another king named Jesus." 8 The
people and the city officials were disturbed when they heard this,
9 and after they had taken bail from Jason and the others, they let
them go.

10 That very night the believers sent Paul and Silas off to Beroea;
and when they arrived, they went to the Jewish synagogue. . . . 13 But
when the Jews of Thessalonica learned that the word of God had
been proclaimed by Paul in Beroea as well, they came there too, to
stir up and incite the crowds.

Paul's Recollection of What Happened

1 Thessalonians 2:1 You yourselves know, brothers and sisters, that our
coming to you was not in vain, 2 but though we had already suffered
and been shamefully mistreated at Philippi, as you know, we had
courage in our God to declare to you the gospel of God in spite of
great opposition. 3 For our appeal does not spring from deceit or
impure motives or trickery, 4 but just as we have been approved by
God to be entrusted with the message of the gospel, even so we speak,

not to please mortals, but to please God who tests our hearts. [5] As you know and as God is our witness, we never came with words of flattery or with a pretext for greed; [6] nor did we seek praise from mortals, whether from you or from others, [7] though we might have made demands as apostles of Christ. But we were gentle among you, like a nurse tenderly caring for her own children. [8] So deeply do we care for you that we are determined to share with you not only the gospel of God but also our own selves, because you have become very dear to us.

[9] You remember our labor and toil, brothers and sisters; we worked night and day, so that we might not burden any of you while we proclaimed to you the gospel of God. [10] You are witnesses, and God also, how pure, upright, and blameless our conduct was toward you believers. [11] As you know, we dealt with each one of you like a father with his children, [12] urging and encouraging you and pleading that you lead a life worthy of God, who calls you into his own kingdom and glory.

[13] We also constantly give thanks to God for this, that when you received the word of God that you heard from us, you accepted it not as a human word but as what it really is, God's word, which is also at work in you believers. [14] For you, brothers and sisters, became imitators of the churches of God in Christ Jesus that are in Judea, for you suffered the same things from your own compatriots as they did from the Jews, [15] who killed both the Lord Jesus and the prophets, and drove us out; they displease God and oppose everyone [16] by hindering us from speaking to the Gentiles so that they may be saved. Thus they have constantly been filling up the measure of their sins; but God's wrath has overtaken them at last.

[17] As for us, brothers and sisters, when, for a short time, we were made orphans by being separated from you—in person, not in heart—we longed with great eagerness to see you face to face. [18] For we wanted to come to you—certainly I, Paul, wanted to again and again—but Satan blocked our way. [19] For what is our hope or joy or crown of boasting before our Lord Jesus at his coming? Is it not you? [20] Yes, you are our glory and joy!

Questions for Careful Reading

10 minutes
Choose questions according to your interest and time.

1 From what various social, ethnic, and religious backgrounds do the first Christians in Thessalonica come? (See Acts 17:1–4; 1 Thessalonians 1:9.)

2 Where does Paul usually preach first when he arrives in a city? Why do you think he starts there?

3 What kind of authority is Paul claiming to have when he insists that the message he preached was not a "human word" but rather "God's word" (1 Thessalonians 2:13)?

4 How does Paul try to avoid being a financial burden on the new church? What drawbacks for the community might result from his arrangement?

5 What do you think it means for the word of God to be "at work in . . . believers" (1 Thessalonians 2:13)? Can you give an example from your own life?

A Guide to the Reading

If participants have not read this section already, read it aloud. Otherwise go on to "Questions for Application."

Acts 17:1–13. Acts reports that after Paul arrives in Thessalonica, he spends three Sabbaths (Saturdays) in the synagogue trying to persuade the local Jewish community to embrace the new Christian faith (Acts 17: 1–3). A number of converts are made, both Jewish and gentile. Then Acts reports next that the apostle is run out of town. Even so, the letters to the Thessalonians seem to imply that Paul has spent considerably longer than three weeks among them. The difficulty is overcome when we recognize that the Acts narrative is highly condensed, with many events intentionally left out to give a brief overview of the Church's earliest days. It simply provides highlights of Paul's experience in Thessalonica. Within the period covered by Acts—probably several months—a number of other events occur as well.

Acts 17:7. Why would the Christians be charged with a political offense simply for practicing their faith? The city of Thessalonica enjoys a favored status granted by the Roman emperor. One way the local citizens maintain their good relations with Rome is through practice of the imperial religious cult, in which the emperor is worshipped as divine. The local authorities and much of the populace view this civic religion as a patriotic duty, a necessary foundation for social and political stability. For this reason, any religious movement that appears to threaten the imperial cult encounters suspicion and animosity.

After conversion, Christians refuse to take part in public rituals honoring the emperor as God. So even though we cannot identify the precise charges against the Thessalonian believers, we can understand at least one motivation behind pagan hostility: when Christians challenge the imperial religious system, they upset the established social and political order.

At the same time, the Christians speak of Jesus as a divine king. Paul later writes that the name of Jesus is "above every name, so that at the name of Jesus every knee should bend . . . and every tongue should confess that Jesus Christ is Lord" (Philippians 2:9–11). Such a statement would have clear political implications for Roman citizens and subjects, who are accustomed instead to thinking of *Rome* as the most exalted

name, to bowing to the emperor, and to declaring "Caesar is Lord!"
So they accuse Christians of divided loyalties.

In an important sense, the Romans are correct. These
new converts now owe their first allegiance to God, and their way
of life clearly challenges the status quo. In future days, when
the will of God and the will of pagan Rome eventually come into
conflict, the Christians will be called to "obey God rather than
any human authority" (Acts 5:29). Their faith will provoke brutal
persecution by the imperial government.

1 Thessalonians 2:1–12. Acts tells us more about how
the missionaries were "shamefully mistreated at Philippi" (1 Thessalonians 2:2): they were dragged by a mob before the authorities for
"disturbing" the city, beaten with rods, and chained in prison (Acts
16:19–24). Despite such "great opposition" (1 Thessalonians 2:2),
Paul forged ahead to Thessalonica.

The apostle seems rather defensive about his ministry.
In this period, traveling philosophers and religious teachers are
common, and many have a reputation for deceit, flattery, laziness,
greed, and immorality. To avoid being identified with such unsavory
people, the apostle reminds the Thessalonians that his conduct
among them was "blameless" (1 Thessalonians 2:10).

1 Thessalonians 2:13–20. Paul's statements here
about the Jewish people sound harsh. But we must keep two truths
in mind. First, the apostle is not speaking about all Jews; after all,
he himself is Jewish—not to mention Jesus, Mary, all the apostles,
and most of the first Christians in Palestine, none of whom are
intended here. In fact, the word translated "Jews" can also be
translated more narrowly as "Judeans," so that Paul seems to refer
specifically to those in Jerusalem and its environs who sought
Jesus' death and violently persecuted his followers, including Paul.

Second, when Paul speaks about the Jewish people as
a whole, he has something positive to say. In his letter to the
Romans, he insists that his "heart's desire and prayer to God for
them is that they may be saved" (Romans 10:1). He urges gentiles
to be grateful to the Jews, to whom they owe many of God's gifts:
the Old Testament Scriptures, worship of the one true God, and
most important, Christ himself (Romans 9:4–5). In the end, Paul
insists, "All Israel will be saved" (Romans 11:26).

Questions for Application

40 minutes
Choose questions according to your interest and time.

1 These biblical texts reflect a troubled history between Jews and Christians that dates back to ancient times. What could you or your parish do to foster reconciliation and mutual respect between these two religious communities?

2 Paul had to defend himself against suspicions and accusations because the misconduct of certain unscrupulous men had soiled the general reputation of religious teachers such as himself. What parallels do you see between Paul's situation and that of Catholic priests and bishops today after the clergy sexual abuse scandals? How can we counter the skepticism of many of our contemporaries toward the clergy?

3 Read again 1 Thessalonians 2:4. Recall an occasion when God tested you by calling on you to speak an uncomfortable truth to someone. Did you pass the test? How did you handle the situation? When has someone spoken an unpleasant truth to you? How did you respond?

2 | *Acts 17:1–10, 13;*
1 Thess. 2:1–20

4 Paul's preaching made costly demands on the Thessalonians to change their lives, yet they still paid the price, accepting the gospel "not as a human word but as what it really is, God's word" (1 Thessalonians 2:13). What specific teachings of the Scripture and the Church have made costly demands on you? Have you been tempted to view any of them as merely human ideas rather than God's word so that you could disregard them?

5 How should American Catholics today respond to civil laws and government policies that they believe are contrary to God's will?

As a key unlocks a door, a question unlocks the mind of group members so they are able to listen to what the Bible says. . . . The discussion which follows a well-placed question will enrich the entire group.

James F. Nyquist and Jack Kuhatschek, *Leading Bible Discussions*

Approach to Prayer

15 minutes
Use this approach—or create your own!

◆ Who among us has never been misunderstood, slandered, or accused unfairly of selfish motives? Paul has more than his share of such injustices. Though understandably angered by such mistreatment, as reflected in his letters to the Thessalonians, nevertheless in his later writings it is clear he has forgiven those who have injured him. Paul prays for his adversaries to be saved (Romans 10:1).

Take a moment to reflect silently on the people who have harmed you through misunderstanding, slander, or unfair accusations. Then pray together the Our Father. After you say, "Forgive us our trespasses as we forgive those who trespass against us," pause to ask God silently to forgive and bless these people. If you feel you have not yet forgiven them yourself, do so now, remembering Paul's instruction: "As the Lord has forgiven you, so you also must forgive" (Colossians 3:13). Then conclude the prayer together.

Saints in the Making

Marcel Van: Refined by Fire

This section is a supplement for individual reading.

Marcel Van was born in 1928 to poor rice farmers in Vietnam. Raised a Catholic, from an early age he showed great interest in religion. So his parents sent him off to work in various parishes as a young boy.

Sadly enough, some of the priests and catechists Marcel worked for abused him physically, and one even tried to abuse him sexually. Other catechists beat him, tempted him to various sins, and taunted him for his devotion to God. Later, he had to deal with several priests who were given to drunkenness and sexual immorality.

At the age of twelve Marcel ran away and took up living on the streets, surviving by his wits, handouts, and sheer stubbornness. At times he was so hungry he ate the drippings of the altar candles. Once he narrowly escaped being sold into slavery.

By God's grace, through all these trials Marcel's love for God remained firm and strengthened. In 1945 he went south to Saigon, where he took vows as a lay member of the Redemptorist religious order. After Communists took control of North Vietnam in 1954, multitudes of refugees fled south to escape the atheist regime. But Marcel heard Jesus say that he was to head back north to serve the people who needed him most.

The young man went to Hanoi immediately to minister spiritually there. Before long he was captured by the Communists, who interrogated him, demanding that he break his religious vows and join their cause. He refused. Convicted of "propaganda against the government," he was sent to two concentration camps, where he was subjected to beatings, months in solitary confinement, and unsuccessful attempts to "reeducate" him through brainwashing. Throughout the ordeal, his courage and endurance gave comfort and strength to the other prisoners.

After a final two years alone in a dark cell, Marcel's thin and weakened body was consumed with tuberculosis and beriberi. He died soon after he was released from isolation, in 1959.

Marcel Van was persecuted for his faith as Paul and the Thessalonians had been. Yet he allowed such adversity to make him stronger. In twentieth-century Vietnam as in first-century Greece, a godly response to suffering provided a shining example—and caused faith and love to abound.

Hold On!

Questions to Begin

15 minutes
Use a question or two to get warmed up for the reading.

1   What's one meaningful family tradition that was practiced in your home when you were a child that you think would be worth passing on to the next generation or to other households?

2   What kind of work do you most enjoy doing with your hands?

Opening the Bible

5 minutes
Read the passage aloud. Let individuals take turns reading
paragraphs.

The Reading: 1 Thessalonians 3:1–4:12;
2 Thessalonians 2:13–17

I Couldn't Stand It Anymore!

1 Thessalonians 3:1 Therefore when we could bear it no longer, we decided
to be left alone in Athens; 2 and we sent Timothy, our brother and co-
worker for God in proclaiming the gospel of Christ, to strengthen and
encourage you for the sake of your faith, 3 so that no one would be
shaken by these persecutions. Indeed, you yourselves know that this is
what we are destined for. 4 In fact, when we were with you, we told
you beforehand that we were to suffer persecution; so it turned out,
as you know. 5 For this reason, when I could bear it no longer, I sent
to find out about your faith; I was afraid that somehow the tempter
had tempted you and that our labor had been in vain.

6 But Timothy has just now come to us from you, and has
brought us the good news of your faith and love. He has told us also
that you always remember us kindly and long to see us—just as we
long to see you. 7 For this reason, brothers and sisters, during all our
distress and persecution we have been encouraged about you through
your faith. 8 For we now live, if you continue to stand firm in the
Lord. 9 How can we thank God enough for you in return for all the
joy that we feel before our God because of you? 10 Night and day
we pray most earnestly that we may see you face to face and restore
whatever is lacking in your faith.

11 Now may our God and Father himself and our Lord Jesus
direct our way to you. 12 And may the Lord make you increase and
abound in love for one another and for all, just as we abound in love
for you. 13 And may he so strengthen your hearts in holiness that you
may be blameless before our God and Father at the coming of our
Lord Jesus with all his saints.

How to Please God

4:1 Finally, brothers and sisters, we ask and urge you in the Lord Jesus
that, as you learned from us how you ought to live and to please God
(as, in fact, you are doing), you should do so more and more. 2 For
you know what instructions we gave you through the Lord Jesus.
3 For this is the will of God, your sanctification: that you abstain

from fornication; 4 that each one of you know how to control your own body in holiness and honor, 5 not with lustful passion, like the Gentiles who do not know God; 6 that no one wrong or exploit a brother or sister in this matter, because the Lord is an avenger in all these things, just as we have already told you beforehand and solemnly warned you. 7 For God did not call us to impurity but in holiness. 8 Therefore whoever rejects this rejects not human authority but God, who also gives his Holy Spirit to you.

9 Now concerning love of the brothers and sisters, you do not need to have anyone write to you, for you yourselves have been taught by God to love one another; 10 and indeed you do love all the brothers and sisters throughout Macedonia. But we urge you, beloved, to do so more and more, 11 to aspire to live quietly, to mind your own affairs, and to work with your hands, as we directed you, 12 so that you may behave properly toward outsiders and be dependent on no one.

Hold Fast to the Traditions

2 Thessalonians 2:13 But we must always give thanks to God for you, brothers and sisters beloved by the Lord, because God chose you as the first fruits for salvation through sanctification by the Spirit and through belief in the truth. 14 For this purpose he called you through our proclamation of the good news, so that you may obtain the glory of our Lord Jesus Christ. 15 So then, brothers and sisters, stand firm and hold fast to the traditions that you were taught by us, either by word of mouth or by our letter.

16 Now may our Lord Jesus Christ himself and God our Father, who loved us and through grace gave us eternal comfort and good hope, 17 comfort your hearts and strengthen them in every good work and word.

Questions for Careful Reading

10 minutes
Choose questions according to your interest and time.

1   What do you think prevents Paul from returning to Thessalonica? Why is it possible for Timothy to go in his place?

2   Reread 1 Thessalonians 4:3–12. If "sanctification" is the process of becoming holy, what aspects of sanctification are specifically identified here by Paul?

3   When Paul says "aspire to live quietly" (1 Thessalonians 4:11), is he speaking simply about being reserved in what we say, or something more?

4   Paul insists he has no need to tell these Christians how to love one another because they have already been "taught by God" how to do so (1 Thessalonians 4:9). What does he mean? (Compare John 15:9–14; Philippians 2:3–11.)

5   Paul instructs the new Christians to "behave properly toward outsiders" (1 Thessalonians 4:12). Why would relationships with non-Christian neighbors be an important concern for these recent converts?

A Guide to the Reading

If participants have not read this section already, read it aloud. Otherwise go on to "Questions for Application."

1 Thessalonians 3:1–13. Separated for perhaps months from his "newborn" spiritual children, Paul was so concerned about them that he sent Timothy back to Thessalonica to check on them. The first letter is written in response to Timothy's report.

The apostle reminds the Thessalonians that persecution is what they are "destined for"; he told them "beforehand" that it was coming (1 Thessalonians 3:3–4). How did he know to brace himself for persecution?

Recall that Paul himself once persecuted Christians before his own conversion. Like many other Jewish religious leaders, he was convinced that Jewish Christians were apostates—traitors to their religion and their people. So he knows well the reasons for their opposition. In fact, Paul's preaching is even more provocative than that of other apostles because he openly challenges certain ancient Jewish traditions and urges Jewish Christians to join spiritually and socially with gentile Christians (1 Corinthians 7:19; 9:20–21; 10:27; Galatians 5:2–6; Ephesians 2:11–19; Colossians 3:11).

Even so, the Thessalonian believers face hostility, not just from their Jewish neighbors but from their "own compatriots" (or "countrymen," 1 Thessalonians 2:14) as well. Why would the Romans, Greeks, and other pagans be so opposed to them?

We have already noted that Christians' withdrawal from the public religious cult of the Roman Empire seems unpatriotic and subversive to their neighbors. But there is more. Worship of the emperor is only one of many religious traditions popular in Thessalonica. Greek gods and goddesses also have their cults here, alongside Egyptian deities. These ancient polytheists (worshipers of multiple deities) usually have no problem making room for one more god in the neighborhood. The more the merrier! But Christians in the ancient world refuse to place a statue of Jesus on the shelf alongside Zeus and Isis. They insist that there is only one true God, the lord and creator of all, and that all other gods are false, even demonic, idols.

Worse yet (in the eyes of pagans), Christians have abandoned the ways of their ancestors for this novel, exclusive religion! They no longer visit pagan shrines, celebrate pagan religious festivals, dedicate children to pagan deities, or consecrate tools in their workshops to the patron gods of their crafts. They socialize across ethnic boundaries; they forgive insults to their honor rather than seeking revenge. No wonder the tensions run high.

1 Thessalonians 4:1–12. Why must Paul address the issue of sexual immorality so firmly? Perhaps Timothy reported that some of the new believers had struggles in this area. At the very least, the admonitions are needed because of the kind of culture from which the converts have come.

Paul warns against being caught up in the "lustful passion" of the pagans (1 Thessalonians 4:5). Though many ancient philosophers in this culture emphasize that reason should guide conduct, the religion of the common people who worship the array of gods we have noted is rarely tied to moral standards. Given that the worship of some of these pagan deities has a strong sexual focus—public processions with lewd images, private orgies with drunken sexual frenzies—the popular culture of this time provides few constraints on sexual promiscuity and disorder.

In contrast to the lust that permeates such a society, Paul refers the Thessalonian Christians to the genuine "love of the brothers and sisters" that God himself has taught them to practice (1 Thessalonians 4:9). One way that love can be expressed is through proper conduct within the community: the believers should "live quietly," "mind [their] own affairs," and "work with [their] hands" (1 Thessalonians 4:11).

2 Thessalonians 2:13–17. Paul says that in the midst of persecution, the Thessalonians can be grateful that God has chosen them for salvation (see also 1 Thessalonians 1:4). We might imagine their responding as did Tevye—the Jewish papa in the Broadway musical *Fiddler on the Roof*—who complained gently to God about the persecution of his religious community, suggesting that maybe sometimes God ought to choose somebody else!

So what is God's purpose in choosing? His people are "a chosen race, a royal priesthood" (1 Peter 2:9)—that is, chosen to become ministers of blessing to the whole world. With this privilege comes responsibility and even suffering. But it is an extraordinary honor nonetheless.

Questions for Application

40 minutes
Choose questions according to your interest and time.

1 Contemporary culture often suggests that it doesn't really matter what we believe as long as we are sincere in our faith. But Paul says that "belief in the truth" actually contributes to our salvation (2 Thessalonians 2:13). Why is correct belief important? Do beliefs have consequences?

2 Some problems Paul mentions in this passage are common today as well: fornication, lust, sexual exploitation. How might we help one another stand firm against the temptations of a sex-saturated culture?

3 Do you think that committed Christians in our society—in particular, Catholics—face opposition because of their faith? Have you ever personally experienced hostility because of your beliefs and practices? How did you handle it? What do you think are the "hot-button" issues in this regard?

4 Christians in several nations today suffer genuine, some-times brutal, persecution for their faith. What can you or your parish do to help these persecuted believers?

5   Today, as in Paul's day, new Catholic converts sometimes face ridicule, rejection, and misunderstanding from loved ones who oppose their decision to embrace our faith. What could you and your parish do to support and encourage such converts?

6   Read again 1 Thessalonians 4:11. In what ways might you learn to live more "quietly" than you do now?

7   Paul's friendship with the Thessalonians is obviously close and intense. What are the advantages and disadvantages of having such a relationship between pastor and parish?

The humble man, however unlearned, is not only potentially, but *already* more a student of God's Word than one who, though scholarly, is proud.

John B. Job, *How to Study the Bible*

Approach to Prayer

15 minutes
Use this approach—or create your own!

◆ One important theme in Paul's letters to the Thessalonians is his desire that they live a life pleasing to God (1 Thessalonians 4:1) so they can have confidence in their readiness to meet Christ at his coming (1 Thessalonians 3:13). That theme figures as well in the following prayer of the great theologian and biblical scholar St. Thomas Aquinas, who lived from about 1225 to 1274. Since he often prayed these words when he studied the Scripture, it would be fitting to pray them now together.

Lord my God, bestow upon me
an understanding that knows
    you,
diligence in seeking you,
wisdom in finding you,
a way of life that is pleasing to
    you,
perseverance that waits trustfully
    for you,
and confidence that I will
    embrace you at the last.
Amen.

A Living Tradition

Is the Scripture Alone Enough?

This section is a supplement for individual reading.

Some Christians insist that Scripture alone must be the source of Church teaching. They believe that any part of the tradition of the Church passed down in a form other than the words written in the Bible—such as the pronouncements of popes and Church councils, canon law, or ancient liturgical practices—has no binding authority. But Paul's statement in 2 Thessalonians 2:15 is one of several showing that such an idea is itself not biblical.

The apostle declares: "Hold fast to the traditions that you were taught by us, *either by word of mouth or by our letter"* (2 Thessalonians 2:15, emphasis added). As the Catholic Church affirms, apostolic authority is not limited to the words in Paul's letters, or even to the Bible as a whole. From the very beginning, the Church has depended on an authoritative and living Tradition of which Scripture is one part, handed down and interpreted faithfully by the official teaching office of the Church. Here is what the Second Vatican Council has to say:

Christ the Lord . . . commissioned the apostles to preach to all men that gospel which is the source of all saving truth and moral teaching, and thus to impart to them divine gifts. . . . This commission was faithfully fulfilled by the apostles who, by their oral preaching, by example, and by ordinances handed on what they had received from the lips of Christ, from living with him, and from what he did, or what they had learned through the prompting of the Holy Spirit. The commission was fulfilled, too, by those apostles and apostolic men who under the inspiration of the same Holy Spirit committed the message of salvation to writing.

But in order to keep the gospel forever whole and alive within the Church, the apostles left bishops as their successors, "handing over their own teaching role to them" (St. Ireneaus, *Against Heresies,* III, 3,1). This Sacred Tradition, therefore, and Sacred Scripture . . . are like a mirror in which the pilgrim Church looks at God, from whom she has received everything, until she is brought finally to see him as he is, face to face (1 John 3:2) (*Dogmatic Constitution on Divine Revelation,* 7).

WHAT ABOUT THE END OF THE WORLD?

Questions to Begin

15 minutes
Use a question or two to get warmed up for the reading.

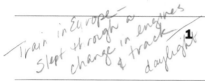

1 What's the most unusual place you've ever fallen asleep? How were you awakened?

2 What is the most memorable unexpected visit you have ever received (or made)? Was it pleasant or unpleasant?

Opening the Bible

5 minutes
Read the passage aloud. Let individuals take turns reading
paragraphs.

Background

This week's readings supplement Paul's words to the Thessalonians with some of Jesus' words from the Gospel of Matthew.
The Gospel passage provides further insight into the apostle's
message about the close of the age.

The Readings: 1 Thessalonians 4:13–5:11;
Matthew 24:36, 42–44

A Thief in the Night

1 Thessalonians 4:13 But we do not want you to be uninformed, brothers
and sisters, about those who have died, so that you may not grieve as
others do who have no hope. 14 For since we believe that Jesus died
and rose again, even so, through Jesus, God will bring with him those
who have died. 15 For this we declare to you by the word of the Lord,
that we who are alive, who are left until the coming of the Lord, will
by no means precede those who have died. 16 For the Lord himself,
with a cry of command, with the archangel's call and with the sound
of God's trumpet, will descend from heaven, and the dead in Christ
will rise first. 17 Then we who are alive, who are left, will be caught
up in the clouds together with them to meet the Lord in the air; and
so we will be with the Lord forever. 18 Therefore encourage one
another with these words.

Children of the Day

5:1 Now concerning the times and the seasons, brothers and sisters,
you do not need to have anything written to you. 2 For you yourselves
know very well that the day of the Lord will come like a thief in the
night. 3 When they say, "There is peace and security," then sudden
destruction will come upon them, as labor pains come upon a
pregnant woman, and there will be no escape! 4 But you, beloved,
are not in darkness, for that day to surprise you like a thief; 5 for you
are all children of light and children of the day; we are not of the
night or of darkness. 6 So then let us not fall asleep as others do, but
let us keep awake and be sober; 7 for those who sleep sleep at night,
and those who are drunk get drunk at night. 8 But since we belong

to the day, let us be sober, and put on the breastplate of faith and love, and for a helmet the hope of salvation. [9] For God has destined us not for wrath but for obtaining salvation through our Lord Jesus Christ, [10] who died for us, so that whether we are awake or asleep we may live with him. [11] Therefore encourage one another and build up each other, as indeed you are doing.

Stay Awake!

Matthew 24:36 "But about that day and hour no one knows, neither the angels of heaven, nor the Son, but only the Father. . . . [42] Keep awake therefore, for you do not know on what day your Lord is coming. [43] But understand this: if the owner of the house had known in what part of the night the thief was coming, he would have stayed awake and would not have let his house be broken into. [44] Therefore you also must be ready, for the Son of Man is coming at an unexpected hour."

Questions for Careful Reading

10 minutes
Choose questions according to your interest and time.

1 Why are labor pains an apt analogy for Christ's return to judge the world (1 Thessalonians 5:3)?

2 What image does the apostle use here to describe the virtues of faith, hope, and love (1 Thessalonians 5:8)? What does that picture suggest in practical terms about the role of these virtues in the Christian life?

3 What seem to be Paul's reasons for teaching and writing about the end of the world? (See 1 Thessalonians 1:10; 2:12, 19–20; 3:12–13; 4:13, 18; 5:2–11, 23; 2 Thessalonians 1:5–12; 2:1–2.)

4 What does Paul mean when he urges us to be "children of the day . . . not of the night" (1 Thessalonians 5:5)?

5 Many people dread the possibility that the world might come to an end. Why does Paul view it as reason for encouragement?

A Guide to the Reading

If participants have not read this section already, read it aloud. Otherwise go on to "Questions for Application."

1 Thessalonians 4:13–18. Paul's initial preaching to the Thessalonians included the promise that the dead will be raised and Christ will come in glory to judge the world. In the apostle's absence, however, confusion has arisen. Perhaps Paul has not given more detailed instruction in this matter before now because of the common expectation that Jesus will be arriving quite soon, in the lifetime of those to whom Paul has preached. But now some of the Christians have died and are no longer on hand for the great event, so new questions have arisen: Will the departed believers miss the Second Coming? Will they have to wait longer than the others to meet Jesus because the Resurrection will take place later?

Paul responds with the assurance that those who have died as Christians will not be forgotten, nor their eternal reward delayed. They will be raised from the dead at Christ's return to join those who are still alive on earth so they can welcome him together.

The apostle is addressing a specific question raised by the Thessalonians, and he has already preached to them on this general subject. So he keeps this description of Christ's second coming short and focused, leading up to one stirring declaration: "We will be with the Lord forever" (1 Thessalonians 4:17). That all-important reality is their source of consolation.

Because Paul's response is brief and ad hoc, we should not look to this passage to offer a complete account of what will happen when Jesus returns. Nor can we expect it to provide us some kind of prophetic "video" of the Second Coming, as if by studying it we can know just how the Lord's arrival will look and sound to the people still living on the earth when he comes. Instead, we must consider the thrust of the passage as a whole.

What overall impression is Paul trying to make? We should note that he resorts to military language to try to describe this mystery (1 Thessalonians 4:16). Jesus will return with a loud command, a summons issued by an archangel, and a (battlefield) trumpet blast. The Lord will arrive, then, in great authority and power, like a conquering warrior king, to rescue his people and execute justice.

It is especially difficult to know which details of this passage should be taken literally and which figuratively. For example,

Paul says believers will "be caught up in the clouds . . . to meet the Lord in the air" (1 Thessalonians 4:17). Will they actually be lifted physically off the ground at Christ's return? Stranger things have certainly happened in the lives of the saints, some of whom have been known to levitate occasionally when encountering the Lord in prayer.

Nevertheless, Paul may simply be using language familiar to Jewish tradition: throughout the Old Testament, when God shows himself to people, his appearance is often described as taking place in bright "clouds," which is a way of describing his exaltation and the radiance of his glory (Exodus 19:16; 24:15–18; 40:34; 1 Kings 8:10–11; Daniel 7:13). To be caught up in the "clouds," then, would be to share the glory of the Lord at his return—a promise Paul makes repeatedly in these letters (1 Thessalonians 2:12; 2 Thessalonians 1:10, 12; 2:14).

In any case, Christ's coming, Paul assures us, will be an event of glorious magnificence. Those who think the Lord could come back unrecognized or unnoticed (as some of the Thessalonians later come to believe) are mistaken. The apostle affirms what Jesus himself declared when he said his return would be like "lightning" across the sky (Matthew 24:27).

1 Thessalonians 5:1–11; Matthew 24:36, 42–44.
Addressing another question, this one about the timing of the Lord's return, Paul writes that we don't know specifically "the times and the seasons" because "the day of the Lord will come like a thief in the night" (1 Thessalonians 5:1–2). His words parallel those of Matthew, in which Jesus says that no one knows "the day and hour" when he will return, compares his coming to that of a burglar who catches a home owner asleep, and tells his disciples to be ready for that "unexpected hour" (Matthew 24:36, 43–44).

Calendars and calculations for this event are thus useless, as numerous failed "end times" movements throughout Church history have demonstrated. (More about this on page 51.) The Lord will take us by surprise! So prepare for him, Paul says, whenever he may come, by living like "children of light"—that is, in a way pleasing to God (1 Thessalonians 5:5).

Questions for Application

40 minutes
Choose questions according to your interest and time.

1 Using figurative language, Paul commands Christians to stay "awake" and "sober" (1 Thessalonians 5:6–11). What do you think it means to be spiritually and morally alert? Can you identify particular situations in your life right now in which you most need this kind of alertness?

2 What are some specific, practical ways that Christians can encourage and build up one another? Which kinds of encouragement and building up do you find yourself needing most often? Which kinds do you most often offer to others?

3 Read 1 Thessalonians 4:13 again. Is Paul forbidding Christians to grieve altogether, or bidding them to do so as people who hope to be with their loved ones again in the Lord's presence? What difference might such a hope of heaven make in the way Christians express their grief?

48

4 If you could know for certain that Jesus would return to earth tomorrow, what would you do differently today? Is there anything you have put off doing that you would want to do before he comes? If so— knowing that the Lord could indeed come at any time—why are you waiting?

5 Extensive end times speculation, both Christian and otherwise, is today promoted through numerous books, videos, and media broadcasts. What do you think is the appeal of such speculation? What are its dangers?

We should read the Bible prayerfully and pray biblically. Since this is God's Word, reading *and* praying it should be part of the same fundamental process.

Peter Kreeft, *Reading and Praying the New Testament*

Approach to Prayer

15 minutes
Use this approach—or create your own!

◆ Sensational speculation about the end of the world can lead to trouble. Yet thoughtful reflection on "the last things," as St. Thomas More, who lived from 1477 to 1535, once observed, can be a "simple medicine" for the soul. Pray together this portion of a prayer Thomas composed as he faced martyrdom:

Give me your grace, dear Lord,
to count the world as nothing;
to set my mind firmly on you . . .
to keep in mind the last
    judgment;
to have ever before my eyes
my death that is ever at hand . . .
to pray for pardon before the
    Judge comes;
to have continually in mind
the passion that Christ suffered
    for me;
to give him thanks unceasingly
    for his benefits;
to redeem the time that I have
    lost until now . . .
to consider as nothing
the loss of worldly goods,
    friends, liberty, life, and all,
for the sake of winning Christ.
Amen.

A Living Tradition

End Times Predictions: A Trail of Tragedy

This section is a supplement for individual reading.

What do the years 200, 380, 838, 1000, 1260, 1534, 1843, 1914, and 1988 all have in common? In each of these years, and many others as well, large numbers of people thought the world would come to an end.

Not surprisingly, the Church has long found it necessary to urge caution in the public teaching of biblical texts about the close of the age. The Fifth Lateran Council (1512–17) specifically forbade the preaching of unorthodox end-times speculations by priests. Why? Because eccentric interpretations of Scripture have provoked tragedy again and again. Here are just three examples:

Eon, an uneducated layman of twelfth-century Brittany, claimed he was the second coming of Christ prophesied in Scripture. He gathered a ragtag army from among the disenchanted poor and terrorized the countryside, plundering, murdering, and leaving countless people to starve to death. The savagery ended only when a band of armed men stopped him.

In 1534 a Dutch Protestant sect took control of the city of Münster, proclaiming it the "New Jerusalem" depicted in the book of Revelation. Their leaders prophesied the imminent end of the world, imposed absolute rule on the city, instituted polygamy, and took a number of teenagers for wives. All who resisted were killed. The city was finally saved by a besieging army.

William Miller, a Baptist lay preacher, predicted that his "calculations" based on various biblical prophecies showed Christ would return in 1843. Tens of thousands of American Christians were persuaded that he was correct; many of them quit their jobs, stopped working their farms, and gave away their possessions to await the Lord's arrival. When Jesus failed to show up, they were devastated. Some were financially ruined; others, feeling spiritually betrayed, gave up their Christian faith altogether.

The lessons to be learned? These misguided prophets were apparently focusing on the wrong biblical texts. These two verses alone, if taken to heart, could have saved them: "First of all you must understand this, that no prophecy of scripture is a matter of one's own interpretation" (2 Peter 1:20). And second, "about that day and hour no one knows" (Matthew 24:36).

APOSTATES AND ANTICHRISTS

Questions to Begin

15 minutes
Use a question or two to get warmed up for the reading.

1 When you were a child, who or what was it that most often kept you from getting into trouble?

2 Who is the most thoroughly evil fictional character you have ever encountered in a book, short story, film, or play? What was the most despicable aspect of the villain's character?

Opening the Bible

5 minutes
Read the passage aloud. Let individuals take turns reading
paragraphs.

Background

This week's readings supplement Paul's words to the
Thessalonians with some of Jesus' words from the Gospel of
Matthew. The Gospel passage provides further insight into the
apostle's message about the challenges facing the Church at
the close of the age.

The Readings: 2 Thessalonians 2:1–12; Matthew 24:3–5, 10–13, 23–25

The Rebellion and the Man of Lawlessness

2 Thessalonians 2:1 As to the coming of our Lord Jesus Christ and our
being gathered together to him, we beg you, brothers and sisters,
2 not to be quickly shaken in mind or alarmed, either by spirit or by
word or by letter, as though from us, to the effect that the day of the
Lord is already here. 3 Let no one deceive you in any way; for that
day will not come unless the rebellion comes first and the lawless one
is revealed, the one destined for destruction. 4 He opposes and exalts
himself above every so-called god or object of worship, so that he
takes his seat in the temple of God, declaring himself to be God. 5 Do
you not remember that I told you these things when I was still with
you? 6 And you know what is now restraining him, so that he may
be revealed when his time comes. 7 For the mystery of lawlessness
is already at work, but only until the one who now restrains it is
removed. 8 And then the lawless one will be revealed, whom the Lord
Jesus will destroy with the breath of his mouth, annihilating him by
the manifestation of his coming. 9 The coming of the lawless one is
apparent in the working of Satan, who uses all power, signs, lying
wonders, 10 and every kind of wicked deception for those who are
perishing, because they refused to love the truth and so be saved.
11 For this reason God sends them a powerful delusion, leading them
to believe what is false, 12 so that all who have not believed the truth
but took pleasure in unrighteousness will be condemned.

False Prophets and Love Grown Cold

Matthew 24:3 When [Jesus] was sitting on the Mount of Olives, the disciples came to him privately, saying, "Tell us, when will this be, and what will be the sign of your coming and of the end of the age?" 4 Jesus answered them, "Beware that no one leads you astray. 5 For many will come in my name, saying, 'I am the Messiah!' and they will lead many astray. . . .

10 "Then many will fall away, and they will betray one another and hate one another. 11 And many false prophets will arise and lead many astray. 12 And because of the increase of lawlessness, the love of many will grow cold. 13 But the one who endures to the end will be saved. . . .

23 "Then if anyone says to you, 'Look! Here is the Messiah!' or 'There he is!'—do not believe it. 24 For false messiahs and false prophets will appear and produce great signs and omens, to lead astray, if possible, even the elect. 25 Take note, I have told you beforehand."

Questions for Careful Reading

10 minutes
Choose questions according to your interest and time.

1 Both Paul's letter (2 Thessalonians 2:7) and Matthew's Gospel (24:12) speak of "lawlessness" in opposition to God. Based on these passages, what does this word mean? Is it more than simple disobedience?

Nostradamus?
Codes in the Bible

2 What kinds of "great signs and omens" might "false prophets" produce (Matthew 24:24), and how would these lead people astray? — *By putting our focus on that and taking it away from doing God's work.*

Both? Evil is and acts just as Love
Through people just as God does

3 In each letter Paul refers to the power and activity of Satan (1 Thessalonians 2:18; 2 Thessalonians 2:9). Is the apostle speaking of an abstraction or a real (non-human) person? What does Paul imply about the nature and limits of Satan's power? (For more information, refer to the *Catechism of the Catholic Church,* sections 391–95.)

4 Why does Paul call lawlessness a "mystery" (2 Thessalonians 2:7)? In what ways is the evil we encounter in the world—its sources, its power, its influence on human beings, including ourselves—beyond our understanding?

It is subtle

A Guide to the Reading

If participants have not read this section already, read it aloud. Otherwise go on to "Questions for Application."

2 Thessalonians 2:1–12. The Thessalonians are confused again. This time, someone is claiming that Jesus has already arrived! The misunderstanding may have come by "spirit" (a recent prophetic utterance), "word" (someone's teaching), or "letter, as though from us" (a forgery claiming Paul's signature) (2 Thessalonians 2:2). Whatever the source, Paul must remind them of what he taught before. The Lord cannot have returned yet because that won't happen until certain other events have occurred: the "rebellion" and the appearance of "the lawless one" (2 Thessalonians 2:3).

If only we knew more about what Paul means here! But we have no surviving texts of his earlier preaching on this subject. At best we can only speculate, as countless Christians have done since the Church's earliest centuries, attempting to connect these statements to other scriptural passages—such as this week's readings from Matthew's Gospel.

Matthew 24:3–5, 10–13, 23–25. Matthew's twenty-fourth chapter is both dazzling and puzzling. Like the book of Revelation, it seems to speak of spectacular events to come just before the end of the world. And also like Revelation, its proper interpretation has long been debated. Just as some scholars think Revelation actually describes circumstances and events of the first century, so some scholars believe that Jesus' prophecies in Matthew 24 (and parallel passages in the other Gospels) were largely fulfilled in AD 70, when the Romans destroyed Jerusalem.

Jesus replies here to a question about when the temple will be destroyed and the end of the world will come, events his disciples apparently assume will coincide. So the traditional interpretation— offered by great Christian teachers such as Augustine and John Chrysostom—is that the Lord's response refers to both events, however distant in time they may be. Some statements in Matthew 24 thus speak of the first-century destruction of Jerusalem, and some speak of Jesus' future return to earth.

From this perspective, the "rebellion" Paul mentions (2 Thessalonians 2:3) has often been identified with the great falling away (rebellion against God) that Jesus prophesies in the Gospel (Matthew 24:10–11). At the same time, the "lawless one" Paul writes about has been typically viewed as the "antichrist" mentioned in John's letters (1 John 2:18, 22; 4:3, 2 John 7). The Greek prefix *anti* means "against" or "in place of," so the antichrist is the opponent of Christ, the false Messiah who tries to take his place—which explains why Paul's description here would bring the term to mind.

Many Christians have concluded as well that the "beast" and the "king" described in Daniel (Daniel 7:19–27; 11:31–39) and the "beast" in Revelation (Revelation 13:1–8) all refer to this shadowy character. (Some of Paul's language actually echoes the Daniel passages, as does Matthew 24:15.) Though entire books have been written attempting to elaborate on the matter, "the one destined for destruction" (2 Thessalonians 2:3) nevertheless remains largely a mystery.

Paul tells the Thessalonians that they already know "what is now restraining" the man of lawlessness (2 Thessalonians 2:6). But the rest of us are still in the dark! Many ancient Christians thought this a reference to the might of the Roman Empire, which they believed was keeping the antichrist from gaining power. Others since then have speculated that it refers to the restraining strength of world governments as a whole, or perhaps even to the Holy Spirit himself. This matter, too, remains a mystery.

Meanwhile, throughout history, Christians thinking they lived at the close of the age have often tried to identify some particular figure of their generation as the antichrist. Candidates have ranged from religious leaders to notorious dictators to famous politicians. We do well to recall here 1 John 2:18: "As you have heard that antichrist is coming, so now many antichrists have come." Perhaps some of these figures, who opposed Christ and persecuted his Church, truly qualified as an antichrist.

Is the antichrist, then, simply a spirit hostile to Christian faith that periodically manifests itself in a demonic political or ideological system? Or is the antichrist an individual appearing in the last days? Perhaps Augustine is right when he concludes that antichrist is actually both: a diabolical hostility to Christ that has emerged repeatedly throughout history will find its ultimate expression in an individual at the close of the age. In any case, Paul's point is clear: Stand firm. In the end, Jesus will be victorious!

Questions for Application

40 minutes
Choose questions according to your interest and time.

---

1 The Thessalonians were "shaken" and "alarmed" (2 Thessalonians 2:2) by teachings claiming to be authoritative but challenging the tradition Paul had passed on to them. So they asked him for clarification. When you find yourself asking what the Church authoritatively teaches about a specific issue, how do you typically resolve the matter?

---

2 What kinds of "false messiahs and false prophets" (Matthew 24:24) lead people astray today? (The *Catechism,* sections 675–77, suggests one kind.)

---

3 Read again 2 Thessalonians 2:10–12. What kind of trouble do we get ourselves into when we love pleasure, comfort, or anything else more than we love the truth? How have you experienced this problem in your own life?

4 Read again Matthew 24:13. Does the Lord save us by offering us an escape from the trials of this world, or by helping us to endure them? Can you provide examples of this truth from your own life? *Both* *Life itself*

5 Perhaps the most telling characteristic of "the lawless one" is that he tries to take God's place (2 Thessalonians 2:4; see also Isaiah 14:12–15, which Christians have tradition- ally interpreted as a reference to the devil). How do we ourselves sometimes try to take God's place in various ways? What happens when we do?

A great deal of spiritual food can be had by asking the basic application questions of any passage of Scripture: Is there an ex- ample for me to follow? Is there a sin for me to avoid? Is there a command for me to obey? Is there a promise to claim? What does this teach me about God and about Jesus Christ? . . . What should be my prayer for today from this passage?

Paul E. Little, foreword to John B. Job, *How to Study the Bible*

Approach to Prayer

15 minutes
Use this approach—or create your own!

◆ In light of Paul's references to Satan and "the evil one" (1 Thessalonians 2:18; 2 Thessalonians 2:9; 3:3), read what the *Catechism of the Catholic Church* (sections 2851–52, 2854) says about the final petition of the Our Father, "Deliver us from evil":

In this petition, evil is not an abstraction but refers to a person, Satan, the Evil One. . . . When we pray to be delivered from the Evil One, we pray as well to be freed from all evils, present, past, and future, of which he is the instigator. In this final petition, the Church brings before the Father all the distress of the world. Along with the deliverance from the evils that overwhelm humanity, she implores the precious gift of peace and the grace of perseverance in expectation of Christ's return.

Now pray the Our Father. After the last petition, recall silently the specific evils you and others you know must face just now, asking for God's protection. Conclude with gratitude for Christ's final victory: "For the kingdom, the power, and the glory are yours, now and forever!"

A Living Tradition

Why Doesn't God Tell Us When Our End Will Come?

St. Athanasius, who lived about 293–373, was a theologian and the patriarch (the equivalent of an archbishop) of the great city of Alexandria, Egypt. He fiercely opposed one of the most powerful threats the Church has ever faced—the Arian heresy, which denied Christ's full divinity—and persevered through many persecutions and exiles imposed by heretical emperors. These words about the end of the world are from his *Third Discourse against the Arians.*

Not to know when the end of the world is, or when the day of the end will come, is actually a good thing for people. If they knew, they might become negligent about the time they have now, focusing their attention instead on the end times. They might even claim that they must focus on themselves alone.

For that reason, God has also been silent about the time when each person will die. If people knew what day they would die, in their relief that it was not yet here they might well neglect to prepare themselves for it throughout most of the days they have remaining.

The timing of both these ends, then—the end of all things and the end of each of us individually—Christ the Word has concealed from us. For the end of all things includes the end of each one of us, and the end of each one of us is, for us, the end of all things. When we cannot be certain about when these things will happen, our destiny is always in view, pulling us forward day by day, so that we reach toward the things ahead and forget the things behind us (Philippians 3:13). . . .

For this reason, when the Savior said, "No one knows about that day and hour" (Matthew 24:36), he added, "Keep awake therefore, for you do not know on what day your Lord is coming" (Matthew 24:42) and "You also must be ready, for the Son of Man is coming at an unexpected hour" (Luke 12:40). He desires that we should always be prepared. . . . Knowing what is good for us better than we do, the Lord established his disciples securely in this right understanding, so that they, being correctly taught, could set right the Christians of Thessalonica when they were likely to run into error on this point.

Now Get Busy!

Questions to Begin

15 minutes
Use a question or two to get warmed up for the reading.

1 With regard to your attitude toward work, where would you rate yourself on a scale of one to ten where one is "relaxed" and ten is "driven"?

2 What is the most physically demanding, mentally strenuous, or emotionally challenging job you have ever held? How long did you last at it?

5 minutes
Read the passage aloud. Let individuals take turns reading paragraphs.

The Reading: 1 Thessalonians 5:12–28; 2 Thessalonians 3:1–18

Some Final Instructions

1 Thessalonians 5:12 But we appeal to you, brothers and sisters, to respect those who labor among you, and have charge of you in the Lord and admonish you; 13 esteem them very highly in love because of their work. Be at peace among yourselves. 14 And we urge you, beloved, to admonish the idlers, encourage the faint hearted, help the weak, be patient with all of them. 15 See that none of you repays evil for evil, but always seek to do good to one another and to all. 16 Rejoice always, 17 pray without ceasing, 18 give thanks in all circumstances; for this is the will of God in Christ Jesus for you. 19 Do not quench the Spirit. 20 Do not despise the words of prophets, 21 but test everything; hold fast to what is good; 22 abstain from every form of evil.

23 May the God of peace himself sanctify you entirely; and may your spirit and soul and body be kept sound and blameless at the coming of our Lord Jesus Christ. 24 The one who calls you is faithful, and he will do this.

25 Beloved, pray for us.

26 Greet all the brothers and sisters with a holy kiss. 27 I solemnly command you by the Lord that this letter be read to all of them.

28 The grace of our Lord Jesus Christ be with you.

Don't Give Up

2 Thessalonians 3:1 Finally, brothers and sisters, pray for us, so that the word of the Lord may spread rapidly and be glorified everywhere, just as it is among you, 2 and that we may be rescued from wicked and evil people; for not all have faith. 3 But the Lord is faithful; he will strengthen you and guard you from the evil one. 4 And we have confidence in the Lord concerning you, that you are doing and will go on doing the things that we command. 5 May the Lord direct your hearts to the love of God and to the steadfastness of Christ.

6 Now we command you, beloved, in the name of our Lord Jesus Christ, to keep away from believers who are living in idleness

and not according to the tradition that they received from us. 7 For you yourselves know how you ought to imitate us; we were not idle when we were with you, 8 and we did not eat anyone's bread without paying for it; but with toil and labor we worked night and day, so that we might not burden any of you. 9 This was not because we do not have that right, but in order to give you an example to imitate. 10 For even when we were with you, we gave you this command: Anyone unwilling to work should not eat. 11 For we hear that some of you are living in idleness, mere busybodies, not doing any work. 12 Now such persons we command and exhort in the Lord Jesus Christ to do their work quietly and to earn their own living. 13 Brothers and sisters, do not be weary in doing what is right.

14 Take note of those who do not obey what we say in this letter; have nothing to do with them, so that they may be ashamed. 15 Do not regard them as enemies, but warn them as believers.

16 Now may the Lord of peace himself give you peace at all times in all ways. The Lord be with all of you.

17 I, Paul, write this greeting with my own hand. This is the mark in every letter of mine; it is the way I write. 18 The grace of our Lord Jesus Christ be with all of you.

10 minutes
Choose questions according to your interest and time.

1 In light of your own experiences in Catholic parishes, what problems do you speculate the church in Thessalonica might be experiencing that would prompt Paul to remind them to respect their leaders (1 Thessalonians 5:12–13)?

apathy

2 Unlike his first letter to the Thessalonians, Paul's second letter repeatedly speaks of giving them a "command" (2 Thessalonians 3:4, 6, 10, 12). Why do you think his tone is firmer now?

3 Reread 2 Thessalonians 2:1–2. Why might Paul take such pains to point out that he has added his own notation (3:17)?

4 Why might some of the Thessalonians who believe the end of the world is at hand be tempted to stop working?

5 Who is it that Paul probably has in mind when he writes of "wicked and evil people" from whom he must be rescued (2 Thessalonians 3:2)?

A Guide to the Reading

If participants have not read this section already, read it aloud. Otherwise go on to "Questions for Application."

1 Thessalonians 5:12–22. Paul concludes his initial letter with a list of brief, rapid-fire directives for community life. First, the people must love and esteem those who labor spiritually among them (1 Thessalonians 5:12–13). These leaders "have charge" of the church "in the Lord"—that is, with Christ's authority and on his behalf. Rather than causing tensions by continually resisting their leadership, the believers should "be at peace" among themselves.

Next, Paul seems to be addressing the leaders themselves, identifying those in Thessalonica who require their special pastoral attention: the "idlers," the "faint hearted," and the "weak" (1 Thessalonians 5:14). Patience is needed with all these new converts. Then turning to the entire church, he warns against common human failings. Instead of getting even when they have been injured, Christians must "do good to one another" (1 Thessalonians 5:15). Instead of worrying or complaining about their troubles, they should "rejoice," "pray," and "give thanks" (1 Thessalonians 5:16–18).

The apostle next focuses on charismatic phenomena—in particular, prophetic utterances. These "spiritual gifts" also appear in the church at Corinth, where Paul has to lay down rules so they will be practiced "decently and in order" (1 Corinthians 12:1–31; 14:1–40). Apparently, the Thessalonians have similar problems.

What is Paul's counsel? Prophecy is a genuine gift of the Holy Spirit, so the church should not "quench the Spirit" by despising "the words of prophets" as a whole (1 Thessalonians 5:19–20). Nevertheless, since not every word that claims to be prophetic is genuine, the church must "test everything" and "hold fast to what is good" (1 Thessalonians 5:21).

Finally, one broad exhortation: "Abstain from every form of evil" (1 Thessalonians 5:22). That pretty much covers it all!

1 Thessalonians 5:23–28. Paul's final blessing on his flock emphasizes that even though he has set high spiritual and moral standards for them, they should not be discouraged by the challenge. God himself is the one who will "sanctify" them (make them holy) "entirely," and because he is faithful, "he will do this" (1 Thessalonians 5:23–24). The apostle humbly asks for their prayers and bids them greet one another "with a holy kiss"

(1 Thessalonians 5:25–26)—perhaps the forerunner of the liturgical "giving of peace" in the Mass.

Paul commands the initial recipients of the letter (probably the church leaders) to read it aloud to the whole community (1 Thessalonians 5:27). This is necessary since many of the believers are probably illiterate, but also because it allows the church to reflect on the apostle's words together as a community.

2 Thessalonians 3:1–18. In the conclusion of Paul's second letter, he repeats his request for prayer, his encouragement that God is faithful, and his expression of confidence that the Thessalonians will receive what he has to say (2 Thessalonians 3:1–4). But he offers one last solemn "command . . . in the name of our Lord Jesus": they must stay away from believers who refuse to work, living instead off the generosity of others (2 Thessalonians 3:6–15).

Paul alluded to this problem in his first letter (1 Thessalonians 5:14); matters seem to have grown worse. The apostle recalls now, as he did then, how he himself offered a good example of laboring hard to provide for himself (1 Thessalonians 2:9–10; 2 Thessalonians 3:7–9). Then he speaks bluntly as he has before: "Anyone unwilling to work should not eat" (2 Thessalonians 3:10). Repeating admonitions he wrote in the first letter, he commands the idlers and "busybodies" to live quietly and work hard (2 Thessalonians 3:11–12). Then he urges the community, even as they separate themselves from those who are disobedient, not to treat them as enemies but as wayward family members (2 Thessalonians 3:15; though this translation has "believers," the Greek word translated here literally means "brothers").

Though the apostle has dictated the letter to a secretary (Timothy?), he writes the last words himself as a personal signature—perhaps because of concerns about forgeries carrying his name (2 Thessalonians 2:2; 3:17). Like the first letter, this one ends as it began, with a prayer for God's grace to rest on Paul's beloved friends (1 Thessalonians 5:28, 2 Thessalonians 3:18).

Questions for Application

40 minutes
Choose questions according to your interest and time.

1 When speaking about prophetic utterances, Paul tells the Thessalonians to "test everything" (1 Thessalonians 5:21). Many Catholics today claim to have received messages from heaven, either in private prayer or through alleged apparitions of Mary. How seriously should we take these claims? How can the Church test them for authenticity?

2 Christians have debated how it's possible to "pray without ceasing" (1 Thessalonians 5:17). In what various ways do you think we could fulfill this command?

3 How is it possible to "give thanks in all circumstances" (1 Thessalonians 5:18) even when our circumstances are tragic?

4 Paul warned the Thessalonian Christians not to repay "evil for evil" (1 Thessalonians 5:15). The word *evil* may lead us to think here about more serious acts of vengeance, but we sometimes want to get even with those who have injured or offended us in small ways as well. What common minor offenses by family members, neighbors, and coworkers are most likely to provoke you to respond in kind? How might you fortify your resolve to respond charitably instead?

5 Paul asks his flock for their prayers (2 Thessalonians 3:1). How often do you pray for your priest, your bishop, and the Holy Father?

6 When do you find yourself most likely to grow "weary in doing what is right" (2 Thessalonians 3:13)? How do you overcome your weariness?

It is one of the glories of the Scripture that it can embrace many meanings in a single passage.

St. Thomas Aquinas

Approach to Prayer

15 minutes
Use this approach—or create your own!

◆ Pray this final prayer together.

God of peace,
thank you for the peace
that comes from our assurance
that you yourself are at work
to make us like your Son, Jesus.

Thank you that your desire
is for us to be ready to meet him
when he comes for us,
whether we meet him at our death
or at the close of the age.

Lord of grace,
give us the grace
to stand firm in faith
and in the face of temptation,
to live a life pleasing to you,
to imitate the steadfastness of
    Christ.

Father, forgive us our failures,
as we forgive the failures of
    others.
Help us to show them the same
    patience
You have shown us.

For you are faithful, Lord,
and worthy of our trust.
We pray to be made worthy
of life forever with you,
and we praise you for your
    goodness,
Father, Son, and Holy Spirit,
Amen.

Saints in the Making

Don't Quench the Spirit!

This section is a supplement for individual reading.

In his *Commentary on First Thessalonians,* St. Thomas Aquinas notes that Paul's words "Do not quench the Spirit" (1 Thessalonians 5:19) apply to many situations. In particular, he suggests that if we would avoid quenching the Spirit, we should be attentive to the Spirit's guidance in everyday matters and follow his lead.

In that light, I will never forget one cool autumn day when my wife, my then four-year-old daughter, and I were raking the huge corner lot surrounding my mother-in-law's home. It held about thirty tall pine trees, and their needles lay thick on the ground. We were half done with the job when my wife let out a groan and shouted, "My engagement ring! It's gone! It fell off somewhere while we were raking!"

The three of us grimly surveyed the large expanse of lawn, then the twelve huge yard waste bags we had stuffed with pine needles. We would have to empty them, one by one, undoing all our work—and even then we might not find the ring. Where to start?

Then my daughter had an idea: "Let's ask God to show us!" I was tempted to dismiss the notion as impractical. But then again, maybe the Spirit was leading her.

"All right," I said. "Let's ask the Lord to show us where the ring is, and then be quiet so we can listen to what he might say." So we sat in a circle on the grass, prayed for help, and remained still just a moment.

Suddenly my four year old jumped up with a big grin. "God told me!" she said triumphantly. Then she pointed to one of the twelve bags. "That one, Dad!" "Open *that* one!"

We had nothing to lose, so I opened the bag. As I did—before I could even pull out any of the needles—the ring came tumbling out.

We stared at the little diamond ring for a few seconds of stunned silence. Then we all broke into a cheer and shouted, "Thank you, Lord!" That day, our daughter taught us all a priceless lesson that both St. Paul and St. Thomas would heartily affirm: Don't quench the Spirit—listen to him!

71

What's This "Rapture" Stuff All About?

Will you be left behind by Jesus when he returns to rescue his people?

That's a question more and more Catholics are being asked these days by Christians who believe in "the rapture." All Christians believe in the glorious return of our Lord to judge the world. The rapture doctrine, however, claims that Christ is coming back not once more but *twice.* The first time, he will secretly snatch away (rapture) true believers from the world to escape the "great tribulation"—a time of natural catastrophes and the antichrist's brutal persecutions. Then, after several years of horror, Christ will return in glory.

Today, many best-selling books and other media products are pushing the "secret rapture" agenda. Perhaps the best known are in the Left Behind fiction series by Tim LaHaye and Jerry Jenkins. These novels have sold many millions of copies in the last few years, and when Catholics read them, they are often left with questions about the end times notions promoted there.

Is the rapture doctrine scriptural? Rapture preachers typically claim that their doctrine comes from the "plain sense of Scripture." What scriptural texts do rapture believers cite to support their belief? One particular passage from 1 Thessalonians is often quoted: "For the Lord himself, with a cry of command, with the archangel's call and with the sound of God's trumpet, will descend from heaven, and the dead in Christ will rise first. Then we who are alive, who are left, will be caught up in the clouds together with them to meet the Lord in the air; and so we will be with the Lord forever" (4:16–17).

The reference here to believers' being "caught up," rapture proponents say, confirms their teaching.

But as we have noted in Week 4, the apostle Paul gives enough details here to make it clear that he is talking not about a secret disappearance of believers but about a magnificent public event: Christ's descent from heaven amid clouds of glory, angels, trumpet blast, and resurrection.

Why would the faithful on earth be "caught up" when Christ arrives this way? According to many biblical commentators since ancient times, Paul uses imagery here reflecting a custom well-known in Roman culture. State dignitaries and victorious generals often made grand public visits to cities. Such an appearance was called by the same Greek term that St. Paul and other biblical writers often used to write about Christ's glorious coming at the close of the age (see, for example, 1 Corinthians 15:23–25).

When the illustrious visitor approached a city with his entourage, he was often met by citizens who went out to welcome him and then accompanied him into the city. In this way they honored the dignitary's arrival and took part in the celebration. The Greek word Paul uses in this passage to describe Christians' going to meet Christ is the same term used for citizens' gathering to meet an approaching celebrity.

In this light, the passage in 1 Thessalonians makes perfect sense. Those who are still alive on earth when Jesus returns will be "caught up" in his clouds of glory to meet him. Then they will accompany him as he enters the world in triumph. This event could hardly be a secret occurrence.

Another text commonly quoted by those who promote belief in a secret rapture comes from Jesus' words in the Gospel: "For as the days of Noah were, so will be the coming of the Son of Man. For as in those days . . . the flood came and swept them all away, so too will be the coming of the Son of Man. Then two will be in the field; one will be taken and one will be left. Two women will be grinding meal together; one will be taken and one will be left" (Matthew 24:37–41).

The assumption among rapture believers is that the man taken from the field and the woman taken from the mill are true believers "caught up" at the secret rapture. The two people left behind, then, are not believers.

As we have noted earlier, there are reasons to conclude that this text applies to Jerusalem's destruction by Romans in the first century, not to the close of the age. But even if we grant that it refers to the end times, we must read Jesus' words carefully. In the days of Noah, who was taken ("swept . . . away"), and who was left? The wicked were taken away in judgment by the flood, and the righteous Noah, with his family on the ark, was left behind in safety. If the rapture teachers are correct in thinking that this passage applies to the close of the age, then it seems to prove the opposite of what they teach about who gets taken and who gets left behind.

Many rapture believers also cite biblical verses that say Christians will be spared God's wrath, such as Paul's statement that "God has destined us not for wrath" (1 Thessalonians 5:9). But when we examine the apostle's references to divine wrath throughout his letters, we find that he is usually referring to everlasting punishment in the next life, not temporary trials in this life. For example, the alternative the apostle presents to being "destined . . . for wrath" is not escape from earthly sufferings but eternal salvation (1 Thessalonians 5:9).

Rapture teachers may respond that the final tribulation under the antichrist, along with various natural catastrophes, is in fact the beginning of the divine wrath that culminates in damnation for those who reject God. But that leads to an inconsistency.

Rapture advocates typically insist that even though true believers will be snatched away, many unbelievers on earth will then come to believe in Christ after that startling event. The rapture advocates must admit, then, that these last Christians *will* have to go through the final tribulation. But if God has truly promised Christians escape from this divine "wrath" of the last days, then why wouldn't the "postrapture" converts escape it as well? As Christians, couldn't they claim the same divine promise for themselves?

Some rapture believers allow that these postrapture converts could somehow be preserved from God's wrath. Maybe he would hide them in places of refuge or they would experience the adversity as purification rather than wrath. But if God can protect Christians still living on earth after the rapture from the final divine wrath, then he has no need to use a rapture to snatch other Christians away as an escape.

In all these ways, then, Scripture fails to support a rapture doctrine. That is why none of the great biblical commentators or theologians throughout Church history, Catholic or Protestant, ever concluded that the rapture idea is taught in the Bible. And that is why the Catholic Church rejects the notion as alien to both

Scripture and Tradition (see the *Catechism of the Catholic Church,* sections 675–77).

Rapture teachers may insist that they are promoting the plain sense of Scripture, but no one seems to have discovered this "plain sense" until modern times. There is no clear historical evidence of such a notion existing before colonial times in America. The doctrine as it is currently taught evolved in the nineteenth century. If it is really contained in Scripture, how could it have escaped the attention of the worldwide Christian community for so many centuries?

This isn't a Catholic-Protestant disagreement. The majority of Protestants throughout history have not believed in a secret rapture. None of the major leaders of the Protestant Reformation ever taught such a doctrine. And many Protestant teachers today reject it. As Robert Gundry, a respected Protestant biblical scholar, has insisted regarding a secret rapture: "The New Testament . . . turns out the lights on that belief by presenting only one return of Christ—after the tribulation."

If the rapture idea is misguided, are there pitfalls for those who believe it? Yes. It offers a false hope. If Christians won't be snatched from the world to escape the great tribulation, then those who expect to be spared will be ill prepared when difficult days actually come.

The secret rapture notion can also lead Christians to give up on trying to improve society. If the world is headed to destruction and God's plan is for his "soldiers" to escape rather than engage the enemy, then why should they bother to fight?

The larger issue here is the place of suffering in Christian life. Rapture teachers often say that Christians are exempt from suffering God's just punishments in this life. They fail to understand that suffering can become a channel of his cleansing grace. We do often suffer because of our sins; but even when we're innocent, our suffering can be joined to Christ's own suffering to cooperate with his redemptive work on earth.

For all these reasons, God has no plan to snatch us out of the world. Instead, the Church will continue her earthly mission until Christ returns in glory.

Suggestions for Bible Discussion Groups

L ike a camping trip, a Bible discussion group works best if you agree on where you're going and how you intend to get there. Many groups use their first meeting to talk over such questions. Here is a checklist of issues, with bits of advice from people who have experience in Bible discussions. (A planning discussion will go more smoothly if the leaders have thought through the following issues beforehand.)

Agree on your purpose. Are you getting together to gain wisdom and direction for your lives? to finally get acquainted with the Bible? to support one another in following Christ? to encourage those who are exploring—or reexploring—the Church? for other reasons?

Agree on attitudes. For example: "We're all beginners here." "We're here to help one another understand and respond to God's word." "We're not here to offer counseling or direction to each other." "We want to read Scripture prayerfully." What do *you* wish to emphasize? Make it explicit!

Agree on ground rules. Barbara J. Fleischer, in her useful book *Facilitating for Growth,* recommends that a group clearly state its approach to the following:

- ◆ *Preparation.* Do we agree to read the material and prepare the answers to the questions before each meeting?
- ◆ *Attendance.* What kind of priority will we give to our meetings?
- ◆ *Self-revelation.* Are we willing to help the others in the group gradually get to know us—our weaknesses as well as our strengths, our needs as well as our gifts?
- ◆ *Listening.* Will we commit ourselves to listen to one another?
- ◆ *Confidentiality.* Will we keep everything that is shared *with* the group *in* the group?
- ◆ *Discretion.* Will we refrain from sharing about the faults and sins of people who are not in the group?
- ◆ *Encouragement and support.* Will we give as well as receive?
- ◆ *Participation.* Will we give each person the time and opportunity to make a contribution?

You could probably take a pen and draw a circle around *listening* and *confidentiality.* Those two points are especially important.

The following items could be added to Fleischer's list:

◆ *Relationship with parish.* Is our group part of the adult faith-formation program? independent but operating with the express approval of the pastor? not a parish-based group?

◆ *New members.* Will we let new members join us once we have begun the six weeks of discussions?

Agree on housekeeping.

◆ *When will we meet?*

◆ *How often will we meet?* Meeting weekly or every other week is best if you can manage it. William Riley remarks, "Meetings once a month are too distant from each other for the threads of the last session not to be lost" *(The Bible Study Group: An Owner's Manual).*

◆ *How long will meetings run?*

◆ *Where will we meet?*

◆ *Is any setup needed?* Christine Dodd writes that "the problem with meeting in a place like a church hall is that it can be very soul-destroying" given the cold, impersonal feel of many church facilities. If you have to meet in a church facility, Dodd recommends doing something to make the area homey *(Making Scripture Work).*

◆ *Who will host the meetings?* Leaders and hosts are not necessarily the same people.

◆ *Will we have refreshments?* Who will provide them? Don Cousins and Judson Poling make this recommendation: "Serve refreshments if you like, but save snacks and other foods for the end of the meeting to minimize distractions" *(Leader's Guide 1).*

◆ *What about child care?* Most experienced leaders of Bible discussion groups discourage bringing infants or other children to adult Bible discussions.

Agree on leadership. You need someone to facilitate— to keep the discussion on track, to see that everyone has a chance to speak, to help the group stay on schedule. Rena Duff, editor of the newsletter *Sharing God's Word Today,* recommends having two or three people take turns leading the discussions.

It's okay if the leader is not an expert on the Bible. You have this booklet, and if questions come up that no one can answer, you can delegate a participant to do a little research between meetings. Perhaps someone on the pastoral staff of your parish could offer advice. Or help may be available from your diocesan catechetical office or a local Catholic institution of higher learning.

It's important for the leader to set an example of listening, to draw out the quieter members (and occasionally restrain the more vocal ones), to move the group on when it gets stuck, to remind the members of their agreements, and to summarize what the group is accomplishing.

Bible discussion is an opportunity to experience the fulfillment of Jesus' promise "Where two or three are gathered in my name, I am there among them" (Matthew 18:20). Put your discussion group in Jesus' hands. Pray for the guidance of the Spirit. And have a great time exploring God's word together!

Suggestions for Individuals

Y ou can use this booklet just as well for individual study as for group discussion. While discussing the Bible with other people can be a rich experience, there are advantages to reading on your own. For example:

◆ You can focus on the points that interest you most.

◆ You can go at your own pace.

◆ You can be completely relaxed and unashamedly honest in your answers to all the questions, since you don't have to share them with anyone!

    My suggestions for using this booklet on your own are these:

◆ Don't skip the Questions to Begin. The questions can help you as an individual reader warm up to the topic of the reading.

◆ Take your time on the Questions for Careful Reading and Questions for Application. While a group will probably not have enough time to work on all the questions, you can allow yourself the time to consider all of them if you are using the booklet by yourself.

◆ After reading the Guide to the Reading, go back and reread the Scripture text before answering the Questions for Application.

◆ Take the time to look up all the parenthetical Scripture references in the introduction, the Guides to the Readings, and the other material.

◆ Since you control the pace, give yourself plenty of opportunities to reflect on the meaning of these letters for you. Let your reading be an opportunity for these words to become God's words to you.

Resources

Bibles

The following editions of the Bible contain the full set of biblical books recognized by the Catholic Church, along with a great deal of useful explanatory material:
- ◆ The Catholic Study Bible (Oxford University Press), which uses the text of the New American Bible
- ◆ The Catholic Bible: Personal Study Edition (Oxford University Press), which also uses the text of the New American Bible
- ◆ The New Jerusalem Bible, the regular (not the reader's) edition (Doubleday)

Books

- ◆ Peter Gorday, ed., "The First Epistle to the Thessalonians," "The Second Epistle to the Thessalonians," in *Colossians, 1–2 Thessalonians, 1–2 Timothy, Titus, Philemon* (Downers Grove, Ill.: InterVarsity Press, 2000).
- ◆ Abraham J. Malherbe, *The Letters to the Thessalonians: A New Translation with Introduction and Commentary* (New York: Doubleday, 2000).
- ◆ Paul Thigpen, *The Rapture Trap: A Catholic Response to End Times Fever* (West Chester, Pa.: Ascension, 2001) and *The Rapture Trap Study Guide* (West Chester, Pa.: Ascension Press, 2003).
- ◆ For more about Marcel Van and other heroic Catholics who have been persecuted for their faith, see Paul Thigpen, *Blood of the Martyrs, Seed of the Church: Stories of Catholics Who Died for Their Faith* (Ann Arbor, Mich.: Charis Books, 2001).

How has Scripture had an impact on your life? Was this booklet helpful to you in your study of the Bible? Please send comments, suggestions, and personal experiences to Kevin Perrotta, General Editor, Trade Editorial Department, Loyola Press, 3441 N. Ashland Ave., Chicago, IL 60657.